Go and Fear Nothing

The Story of Our Lady of Champion

Patrick O'Hearn

Illustrated by
Ann Kissane Engelhart

Huntington, Indiana

Theoni Bell, author of *The Woman in the Trees*, provided invaluable feedback on the manuscript and illustrations.

Every reasonable effort has been made to determine copyright holders of excerpted materials and to secure permissions as needed. If any copyrighted materials have been inadvertently used in this work without proper credit being given in one form or another, please notify Our Sunday Visitor in writing so that future printings of this work may be corrected accordingly.

Our Sunday Visitor Publishing Division
Our Sunday Visitor, Inc.
200 Noll Plaza
Huntington, IN 46750
www.osv.com
1-800-348-2440

ISBN: 978-1-63966-050-6 (Inventory No. T2801)
LCCN: 2023936490
Cover and interior design: Lindsey Riesen
Cover and interior art: Ann Kissane Engelhart

1. JUVENILE NONFICTION—Religious—Christian—Biography & Autobiography.
2. JUVENILE NONFICTION—Religious—Christian—General.
3. RELIGION—Christianity—Catholic.

PRINTED IN TURKEY

This book is lovingly dedicated to my
daughter, Mella Rose Marie.

Marie Brise was born on January 30, 1831, in a country called Belgium. Her parents called her Adele. As they looked at their baby girl, they never dreamed that someday the Mother of God would give her an important task. Her work would touch many souls.

Adele's parents taught her to love Jesus and Mary very much. When Adele received her first holy Communion, she thought about Jesus' great love. In the Eucharist, the God who made everything chose to make himself small. He made himself look like bread and wine so he could be close to her. Adele was so thankful for this gift from God. She and some of her friends promised Jesus' mother, Mary, that they would all one day join the religious sisters who taught them and serve in a distant country. They would tell others about God.

Life was not easy for Adele. When she was still little, her eye was burned by lye, which was used for making soap. After the accident, she was blind in her right eye. People stared at her everywhere she went. Adele struggled to study and to help her family on their farm because working with one eye is very difficult.

One year, another hard thing happened in Adele's life.
Her parents said, "We are moving to America." They were
excited. Adele and her two sisters were surprised. *What does
this mean?* Adele thought to herself. She told her parents that
she would not go to America. Adele remembered the promise
she made with her friends. If she left Belgium, how could she
become a religious sister with them?

She prayed and spoke with her priest. He told her to go with her family. The Brise family boarded a ship to America in 1855. Adele felt afraid to leave the country where she was born. She did not know how she would become a religious sister in America, but she remembered what the priest said: "If God so willed, she could be a sister in America."

God and Our Lady were with her on the journey.
The ship sailed across the mighty, blue Atlantic
Ocean. It was the biggest, deepest, and widest
body of water Adele had ever seen.

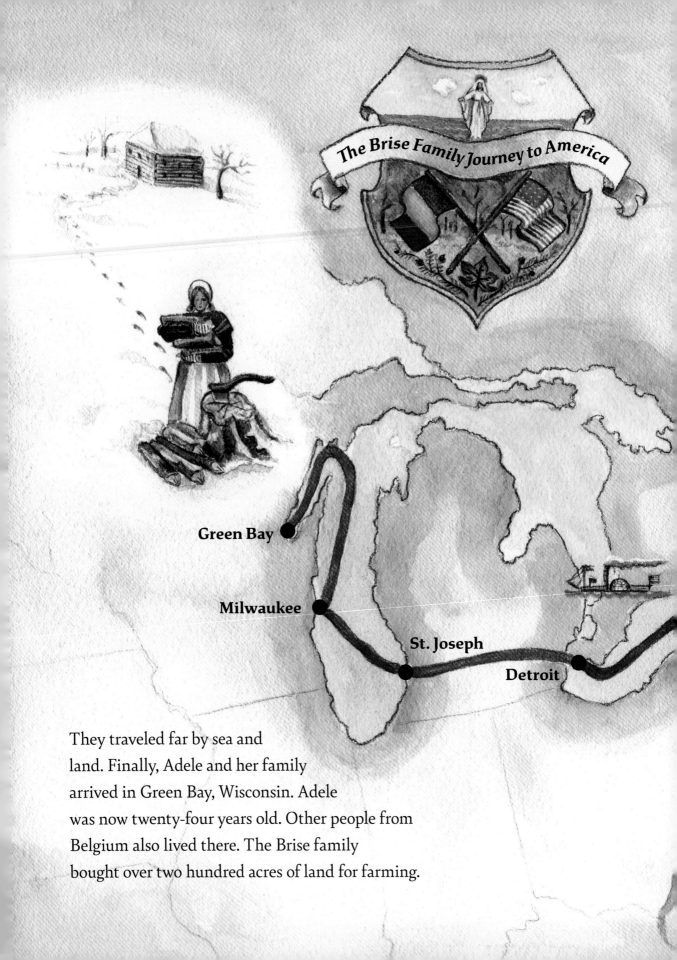

The Brise Family Journey to America

Green Bay

Milwaukee

St. Joseph

Detroit

They traveled far by sea and
land. Finally, Adele and her family
arrived in Green Bay, Wisconsin. Adele
was now twenty-four years old. Other people from
Belgium also lived there. The Brise family
bought over two hundred acres of land for farming.

Every day, Adele felt a little more at home in Wisconsin. But it was still hard to get used to the cold winters! Adele wondered what God was calling her to do in America. She prayed often that God would guide her. She never forgot what the priest back home had told her. If God wanted her to become a religious sister, he would make it happen. She had no idea her life was about to change forever.

Albany

Buffalo

New York City

One October day in 1859, Adele took wheat to the mill to make flour. As she walked, she saw a lady in white floating between a maple and a hemlock tree. Adele froze in fear. She then dropped to her knees in amazement at the lady's presence. She was more beautiful than the sparkling, blue waters of the sea. Unfortunately, the lady left before Adele could find out who she was.

Adele hurried home to tell her parents about the mysterious lady in white. Adele thought to herself, *Who could this lady be? I hope my parents believe me.* Adele's parents did believe her. They thought it might be a poor soul in purgatory seeking her prayers.

Adele wanted to meet the lady in white again and find out who she was. She could not stop thinking about the lady. Would she appear again? Where would she be this time? Between the two trees? Or would she appear in the open fields, or even over the waters of the bay?

A few days later, Adele walked to Mass on the
same path. Her sister Isabelle and a neighbor
were with her. Suddenly, Adele saw the lady in
white again! Once again, the lady said nothing.
She was only visible to Adele — Isabelle and
the neighbor could not see the lady.

Adele thought to herself, *Who is this
lady and what does she want from me?
Is she a poor soul in purgatory, or someone
from heaven? I wish others could see her.*

Troubled by this second vision, Adele went to confession
and Holy Mass. She asked her parish priest, Father Verhoef,
for advice. What should she do if the lady in white appeared
again? Father told Adele to say, "In God's name, who are you
and what do you want of me?"

As Adele walked home from Holy Mass with her sister and neighbor, she recited Father Verhoef's words to herself. She wanted to be ready.

The beautiful woman appeared to Adele for a third time. The lady was clothed in dazzling white, with a yellow sash around her waist. Her dress fell to her feet in graceful folds. She had a crown of stars around her head, and her long, wavy, golden hair fell loosely over her shoulders.

Adele knelt and asked the lady, "In God's name, who are you and what do you want of me?"

In a most gentle voice, the lady said, "I am the Queen of Heaven, who prays for the conversion of sinners, and I wish you to do the same. You received holy Communion this morning, and that is well. But you must do more. Make a general confession, and offer Communion for the conversion of sinners. If they do not convert and do penance, my Son will be obliged to punish them."

"Adele, who is it?" asked Isabelle.

"Oh, why can't we see her as you do?" cried their neighbor.

"Kneel!" Adele replied. "The lady says she is the Queen of Heaven."

Our Lady looked kindly at Adele's companions and said, "Blessed are they that believe without seeing."

Then, she turned back to Adele and said, "What are you doing here in idleness while your companions are working in the vineyard of my Son?"

Teary-eyed, Adele asked, "What more can I do, dear lady?"

Our Lady answered, "Gather the children in this wild country and teach them what they should know for salvation."

Adele stared at the ground. She had very little education herself. Finally, she raised her eyes to Our Lady and asked, "But how shall I teach them who know so little myself?"

Full of love, Our Lady said, "Teach them their catechism, how to sign themselves with the Sign of the Cross, and how to approach the sacraments; that is what I wish you to do. Go and fear nothing. I will help you."

As Our Lady departed, she lifted her hands. She seemed to be asking someone to bless Adele and her three companions. Who was that someone? It could only be her Son, Jesus! From this point on, Adele knew her life would never be the same. She must do God's will, no matter the cost.

With her priest's blessing, Adele set off to teach the catechism to the children. She walked from one village to the next. She walked through sun, rain, and snow, and through forests filled with black bears and wolves.

Many people couldn't wait to meet the woman who saw Our Lady. Others thought she was lying. Still others were scared of her injured eye.

Adele prayed that these parents would let her teach their children about Jesus and Mary. And if they did, she would help them with their chores.

Adele's father also wanted to assist Our Lady. He built the first chapel to Our Lady on the very spot where she had appeared to Adele.

Some women wanted to help Adele teach the children. So Adele started a community called the Sisters of St. Francis of Assisi. They were a third order of sisters. This means that they dressed like nuns, but they did not take official vows. Thus Adele's dream of becoming a religious sister finally came true.

Several years later, the sisters founded St. Mary's Academy next to the chapel. The sisters would care for orphans and teach the Faith. The days of walking fifty miles in the wilderness were over. The sisters were not as young as they used to be.

At St. Mary's Academy, the sisters welcomed the children with open arms. The children were very happy. The sisters taught the children to pray and sing hymns to Our Lady. They also learned math, writing, and French. They worked so hard!

On October 8, 1871, a giant fire broke out in the northern woods. To
escape the raging fire, some people jumped into the rivers and lakes.
Others called upon God to help them. The fire was so strong that it
leaped across the bay. It was headed for the chapel and school, more
than sixty miles from where it began.

Seeing the tall flames and smoke, the sisters rushed
the orphans to the chapel. The scared children held
on to the sisters' habits. The children remembered
what Sister Adele had always told them: "Our Lady
said, 'Go and fear nothing. I will help you.'"

The fire was so great that people thought the world was ending. Many families fled to the holy place where Mary appeared to Adele. Some even brought their farm animals to the property.

In the tiny chapel, everyone asked God and Our Lady to protect them. They prayed the Rosary and carried a statue of Mary all through the night.

In the morning, rain burst from the sky. God had heard the people's prayers. The rain put out the fire, saving the school, the chapel, and the six acres dedicated to Our Lady. It was the only piece of land completely untouched by the fire for hundreds of miles.

The people cried tears of joy and thanksgiving to God and Our Lady. The date was October 9, 1871. It was a miracle, and many more would come!

Today, pilgrims visit the National Shrine of Our Lady of Champion in Champion, Wisconsin, where Our Lady appeared to Adele. Many of them are still seeking miracles.

While many years have passed since Our Lady appeared to Sister Adele, Our Lady's message is more important than ever. Our Lady asks of us what she asked from Adele. She wants us to pray for the conversion of sinners. She wants us to learn our catechism. She wants us to receive the sacraments with great love. And she wants us to rely on her help. When we doubt ourselves, let us remember Our Lady's words to Adele: "Go and fear nothing. I will help you."

Our Lady of Champion, *pray for us!*

Prayer to Our Lady of Champion

by Patrick O'Hearn

Our Lady of Champion and
Queen of Heaven, I love you.

Help me to love your Son as you do.

Help me to love the sacraments and
share them with others.

Help me to teach the catechism to others.

Help me to care for the orphans
and the forgotten.

Help me to pray for the conversion of sinners.

Help me to follow God's will above everything.

Help me to fear nothing, for you are with me.

Amen.

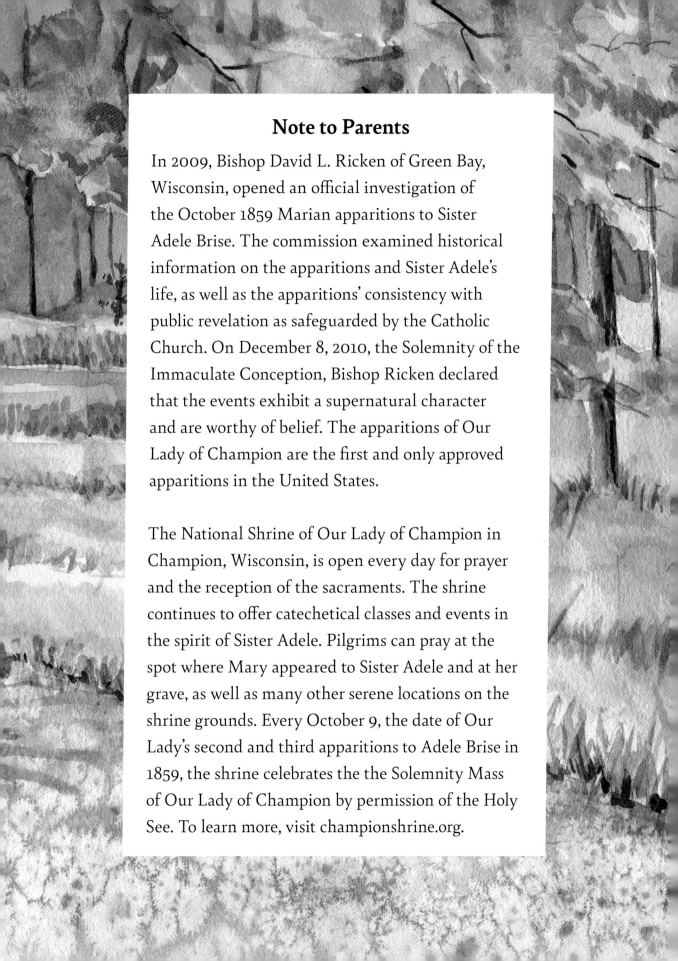

Note to Parents

In 2009, Bishop David L. Ricken of Green Bay, Wisconsin, opened an official investigation of the October 1859 Marian apparitions to Sister Adele Brise. The commission examined historical information on the apparitions and Sister Adele's life, as well as the apparitions' consistency with public revelation as safeguarded by the Catholic Church. On December 8, 2010, the Solemnity of the Immaculate Conception, Bishop Ricken declared that the events exhibit a supernatural character and are worthy of belief. The apparitions of Our Lady of Champion are the first and only approved apparitions in the United States.

The National Shrine of Our Lady of Champion in Champion, Wisconsin, is open every day for prayer and the reception of the sacraments. The shrine continues to offer catechetical classes and events in the spirit of Sister Adele. Pilgrims can pray at the spot where Mary appeared to Sister Adele and at her grave, as well as many other serene locations on the shrine grounds. Every October 9, the date of Our Lady's second and third apparitions to Adele Brise in 1859, the shrine celebrates the the Solemnity Mass of Our Lady of Champion by permission of the Holy See. To learn more, visit championshrine.org.

Helping families love and live the Catholic Faith

OSV Kids is an exciting new brand on a mission to help children learn about, live, and love the Catholic Faith. Every OSV Kids product is prayerfully developed to introduce children of all ages to Jesus and his Church. Using beautiful artwork, engaging storytelling, and fun activities, OSV Kids products help families form and develop their Catholic identity and learn to live the faith with great joy.

OSV Kids is a monthly magazine that delivers a fun, trustworthy, and faith-filled set of stories, images, and activities designed to help Catholic families with children ages 2-6 build up their domestic churches and live the liturgical year at home.

OSV Kids books are crafted to inspire and delight kids and parents alike. Each book is designed to kindle the Catholic imagination within young readers through creative storytelling, stunning artwork, and fidelity to the Church's teachings. With board books for infants and toddlers, picture books for young readers, and exciting stories for older kids, OSV Kids has something for everyone in your family.

Learn more at OSVKids.com

About the Author

Patrick O'Hearn is an author and editor. He has authored or coauthored six books, including the *Parents of the Saints, Nursery of Heaven* (coauthor), *The Shepherd at the Crib and the Cross, Courtship of the Saints, The Grief of Dads* (coauthor), and *Go and Fear Nothing*. His subjects of interest include the lives of the saints and the interior life. You can visit his website at contemplativeheartpress.com.

About the Illustrator

Ann Kissane Engelhart is an accomplished watercolor artist, illustrator, and educator. *Go and Fear Nothing* is her tenth illustrated book. She illustrated *The Light of Christmas Morning* by Susan Bellavance. Ann has worked with Amy Welborn to produce the children's books *Friendship with Jesus, Be Saints!, Bambinelli Sunday,* and *Adventures in Assisi*. She collaborated with Nancy Brown and Regina Doman on *The Chestertons and the Golden Key*, and with Donna-Marie Cooper O'Boyle on *Our Lady's Message to Three Shepherd Children and the World* and *Christmas Joy with Grandma*. Her portraits, still-life and landscape paintings are featured in galleries and private collections. Ann lives in New York with her husband and has two grown children.